Diminishing Secrets
of Zephyrrine

Kitty Hyatt

Presentation by *BookLeaf Publishing*

Web: www.bookleafpub.com

E-mail: info@bookleafpub.com

ISBN: 9789357440042

First edition 2023

PREFACE

Steady as the seasons pass. Growth and rebirth. Death and destruction.

2015 ~ Zephyr

Veneration

You are beautiful, My Love.
But you can't save my soul."

"You are beautiful, My Love.
But I can't save your soul."

"You are beautiful, My Love.
But I can't help my soul."

You are beautiful, My
love, but this is my war.

You are beautiful, my love. Thank
you for the support.

You are beautiful, my love;
shelter yourself from the storm.

A-romantic

I look at you and I feel a flutter.

You look back and it's gone.

But it was beautiful while it lasted.

You were a mountain of words and primal beauty.

You were a dream until you looked at me.

Until you saw me with Eros-filled eyes and expectations.

When you saw that I was a real person.

You noted that I existed and that I was the artist and the canvas;

The student willing to learn.

But you wanted me to guide you. You needed me to lead you.

And I was not placed here to be your instructor.

I was not put here to be on the pedestal above you.

I am your peer. We grow together.

We learn.

We explore.

We process the hard words, the concepts that don't make sense because "Why can't we just love for sake of being a person, a place, or a thing with value."

Why is it not liberating? We should feel our deliverance when we utter those words, not the feeling that everything is dependent and repressive.

Love is power.

Love is strength.

Love is real-life magic.

Love comes in many shapes and forms just like the people that walk this earth.

Love is -romantic.

Love is alterous.

Love is fire and passion that is that moment, not forever.

Love is that flutter while it last and you are responsive and thankful.

"Praise be!" you shout from the only place that you understand.

Your unfamiliarity? Your unawareness?

Fuck! You have made me a goddess.

Another pedestal I will fall from.

But it was beautiful while it lasted.

Try not to Fall

That moment when you know you are breaking.

I've been holding it together for so long that it's just really hard now.

What do you do when you realize that everything you do is wrong?

That nothing you do will ever be good enough.

Well in real life you just can't stop, so I'll just have to keep moving and try not to fall.

Head Thy Objection to Distraction

Darkness, Evil, VILE, unadulterated darkness.

Who lurks behind the shadows blackened by
hated despair?

He who watches us from his lofty throne, hollow
body staring.

Servants feeding off the pain of those whose
souls are being slashed

and dragged into the heated abyss.

Shining so bright with light so inviting that fear
does not enter until you

breach the golden shine to find blackness in its'
belly.

I, Love, You

Three innocent words.

 I, love, and you combined are a deadly force.

Used in personal gain.

Used in truth.

" I love you"

Such an unfaithful vow.

I've heard it so many times.

Said it just as often, when I thought the feeling
was there.

How can I trust myself or anyone else, when
I've hurt others and they've hurt me with those
words?

Stop me

I hate everything about me,

but still, I don't grieve.

All passions are spent and most deceived.

That is the most worldly decree.

And who will save us from ourselves;

On whom will rely?

When our hearts are dark and our souls are not pure,

how can we endure?

I don't understand the many truths and secrets of these vast lands,

but the pain is beginning to seep through my cracked armor.

I try so hard to hide the hurt deep inside.

Years of this unbearable emotion are bubbling
forth.

No beauty lies here.

Ugliness hidden behind paint is all you see.

Please help me.

Tell me what to do, what to change.

But you can't when all your passions are spent
and most deceived.

Who will save me from myself?

On whom shall I rely?

Who will save us now?

Who will save me now?

Stop me now!

I forgot

I spent so much time protecting you, loving you, defending you, that I almost forgot myself.

Let me be.

Let me want me.

I'll rise for me.

A Cutters Breakdown

I'm falling, spiraling into a heated abyss.

The pain has burned and scarred my skin.

Love non-apparent in my circle;

The cold razor slides across my skin,

eager to end the exhilarating sensation.

Senses clouded. An intoxicating scent. Passion igniting;

Wanting to trust but unable to.

Wondering, is it a lie? A beautiful lie;

I don't need or want another letdown leading to another meltdown.

I hold my savior, my friend, waiting for the courage to break that promise.

Unfaithful promise.

I'm coming to my end.

Don't be like me

Don't look up to me.

Don't want to be me.

Don't want a life like mine.

You don't want what it takes to get to where I am.

You don't want the twisty, malevolent heart.

You don't want plastic smiles.

You don't want the darkness.

Not all the shinies are good.

Don't be like me, because I am scary.

Be like you.

Find your truth.

Find you.

Find your shiny.

Alone

Empty, laughing infectiously
at the fate that has left me,
alone in this void.
Prying of my Heart unceasing
to leave me empty.

Dry, tear tracks like an evaporated river left
curiously,
Now no one will ever see
alone here in this dark void. Cold yet sweet
caressing
to leave me alone in my place and empty.

They are coming, Laughing to take me away
But yet I have already been, cut, torn, Slain.
Such gripping fear of love, lust, my own internal
fear, the
feel of those madmen at my heels,
has driven me into my darkness, destroying me
from my insides out.

Begging for peace only brings pleasure to them,
those hounds breathing so close to me.
Yes, I am afraid, Deathly afraid.

Afraid because I am stuck here with the
deafening laughter,
ALONE.

Purposely

Let me know, my lover,
When I need to go, my dear.
I love you so,
but I can't be the woman of your dreams.

Love is beautiful.
It comes in many shapes and forms.
Love is unique,
For me, there are no templates on repeat.

I've shed my skin,
I've looked within
And shattered my very core.

I won't back down,
I can't stop now.
I'm free.

Your amorous canvas is set,
Already painted red.
Your pigment choice is bold
Which retail selection, holiday collection
Was your inspo board?

Let's try something new

A deconstruction tool.
No, that's not what I mean.
Just breathe and
Take a moment to connect.

I'll add some black, some splotches of green.
What will we create?
You try now.
Mountains, sturdy and sound.
Our creation has grown.

The symbols well round,
Show our foundation.
Strong, living, allied.

Let me know, my lover,
Do I need to go, my friend?
I can love you, but not the way you dream.

Being Invisible

I'm there sitting in front of you, having a
discussion, debate, argument,
but I'm invisible.
You see my corporal self, but you ignore who I
am if it doesn't conform to the me you picture.

I'm just a ghost dancing along in this plane until
it's time to move on.
What happened to being who you are?
It's a lie we are fed.
A Hypocrisy that this society is reinforced with.
Be yourself as long as it's a self we approve of.
And what does this breed?

Death, Silence, Pain, Suffering, Fear, Crying,
Desperation.

The hole in my brain

What is this place?

Pure imagination?

A thought?

A feeling?

Uncontrollable measures?

Maddening to the point of no return.

Painting Reality

We are creating art with our love and feelings
for each other.

Every touch.

Every moment.

Each painting has a different style…

because of you.

Communion

Relationships are about communication.
But what is that?
An autonomous self, resource sharing.
Interaction.
Enjoying the human experience both in parallel
and cooperative nature.
A joining of confessions enshrined in grace.

Many

Poly

Means many.

Means sides.

Means overwhelmed.

Means emotions.

Means shapes.

Polyamory means love.

Means heartbreak

Means disappointment.

Means changed plans.

When that goddess warrior you love is dead.

Means more.

Means chances.

Means exploration.

Because you've opened your world to so many different experiences.

Means learning.

Means self-love.

Means self-care.

Means being open.

Polyamory means being scared, but being brave enough to open yourself up on varying levels over and over again.

Means teaching the world to love.

Coded

Growth. Healing.

It is all necessary.

In our world, we focus so much on the self
rather than the whole.

"Grow"...
but not too much. Just enough that I am not
ashamed of you, but not enough that I am
intimidated by you.

"Heal"...
but not in a way that you hold them accountable,
just enough that you internalize what's
happening.

"Heal", because they fear the entirety of the
human emotional experience.
"Heal" because you are different.

No.

Heal because we are connected.
Heal because we liberate ourselves.

That is our growth

Take Space

Not caring doesn't help anyone, much less yourself.

It teaches you to bottle up the negatives until it becomes too much.

We are stunting our interpersonal development.

Taking space is a boundary.
Ignoring a situation long-term is an unhealthy coping mechanism.
Decide how much space you need.

If you were ever my friend…

You shouldn't feel honored, but you should
know just how important that one word is.

You see "friend" is a term that reminds me of
self-decomposition.

Friendship for so long was the same as control
and manipulation and

"if you don't conform you are worthless"

"Friend" has been that rolling duffel bag version
of baggage that I construct and reconstruct
almost as much as I do the term family.

I learned that I can choose my family and cut off
the toxic bits that were poisoning me and
contributing to my timely demise.

I learned friend was a choice, something
precious that not everyone gets to hold, no
matter how much they demand it.

"Friend," I say it again "Friend".

I have deemed you worthy.

I do not consider you a person to wear one of my
countless faces around.

No pretty painted mask.

If I consider you my friend, and that is the
distinction.

You witness my dark, my grim as I dance around
in a pretty white lace dress and canvas shoes, the
epitome of decay-covered innocence, with my
afro puffs standing tall against the users and
abusers, bubbles in hand.

Bubble kisses so sweet cause I took down a
brick so we pass notes back and forth.

I called you my friend and meant it.

Proclimation

I have a voice and it is loud.

Some people don't like it because I have learned
to be proud.

I like my voice, well I do now.

I like my voice because now I stand up for me.

I will not allow you to push me into your box.

So that means I am not humble.

I am not humble and I will gladly take it.

I am not humble because I fought and found
value in myself and my words.

I am not humble because I developed a sense of
dignity.

I have a voice and all you wanted me to have
was a meager sense of self when you said it was
ok to speak as long it was in alliance with your
view.

And no I do not accept your view.

I do not accept your objectification, erasure, or manipulation.
I do not accept your worship that says so you should die.

I do not accept your "well-meaning" prayers or blessing to purge me of my demons, because of those demons, that sin is my light.

I bask in that glory.

I will be loud and proud and when you try to bury me, I will climb high and shout from the rooftops I have to.

I am here.

I am here.

I am here and you will hear me.

Intervene

Intervene.

Sometimes people need help.

To be safe. To not cause harm. To heal.

Societies are social. We need to remember that isolation makes none of us better. Ignoring something doesn't make it go away.

It is your business. Your communities being healthier is your business. Do something about it even if it is the small change of reaching out to one single person.

Small acts are not as insignificant as they seem.

xox, kitty